Formula One
RACING

By Brant James

SportsZone

An Imprint of Abdo Publishing
www.abdopublishing.com

www.abdopublishing.com

Published by Abdo Publishing, a division of ABDO, PO Box 398166, Minneapolis, Minnesota 55439. Copyright © 2015 by Abdo Consulting Group, Inc. International copyrights reserved in all countries. No part of this book may be reproduced in any form without written permission from the publisher. SportsZone™ is a trademark and logo of Abdo Publishing.

Printed in the United States of America, North Mankato, Minnesota
032014
092014

THIS BOOK CONTAINS
RECYCLED MATERIALS

Cover Photo: Rob Griffith/AP Images
Interior Photos: Rob Griffith/AP Images, 1; Gero Breloer/AP Images, 4–5; Ron Hoskins/AP Images, 7; Michael Conroy/AP Images, 11; Felipe Dana/AP Images, 13; Everett Collection/Shutterstock Images, 14–15; AP Images, 17, 40; Girolamo di Majo/AP Images, 19; Shutterstock Images, 20, 32–33; David Acosta Allely/Shutterstock Images, 22–23; Natursports/Shutterstock Images, 25, 26, 30–31; Lori Carpenter/Shutterstock Images, 28; Anton Gvozdikov/Shutterstock Images, 34; Jens Buettner/AP Images, 36; Remo Nassi/AP Images, 38–39; Gilbert Tourte/AP Images, 43; Armando Franca/AP Images, 44

Editor: Patrick Donnelly
Series Designer: Craig Hinton

Library of Congress Control Number: 2014932865

Cataloging-in-Publication Data
James, Brant.
 Formula One racing / Brant James.
  p. cm. -- (Inside the speedway)
Includes bibliographical references and index.
ISBN 978-1-62403-403-9
1. Automobile racing--Juvenile literature. 2. Grand Prix racing--Juvenile literature. I. Title.
796.72--dc23

                                                                    2014932865

TABLE OF CONTENTS

THE GREATEST GETS GREATER

Patience is difficult for race car drivers. To them, patience seems unnatural. Drivers are possessed by the desire to get to the front and to get there quickly. They want to stay in front no matter the cost. Anyone who gets in their way or tries to catch them is the enemy.

Michael Schumacher followed those impulses. They helped make him a great Formula One racer. But he did not become

Michael Schumacher takes the checkered flag at the US Grand Prix in 2003.

the best in the world until he learned the value of patience. It all came together one rainy afternoon.

Schumacher had five Formula One titles by the summer of 2003. Only two races remained in the season. Winning another race would be tough. He was leading the driver standings by a tiny margin. But he was not performing well under pressure. Juan Pablo Montoya was pushing Schumacher hard. A lot was on the line at the legendary Indianapolis Motor Speedway. The racers' fate would be decided at the track known as "The Brickyard."

Schumacher and his red Ferrari came to Indianapolis, Indiana, needing a strong finish. This was an unfamiliar position for the German driver. He had spent much of his career beating his rivals easily.

Things looked even worse before the race started. Schumacher had not run a great qualifying lap. The qualifying

lap determines at which position a driver starts a race. He would start behind most of the drivers attempting to beat him for the championship. They had been faster in their qualifying laps.

The brash and talented Kimi Raikkonen from Finland was on the pole. That meant he would start at the front of the line as the fastest qualifier. Doing so can be a huge advantage. With no one in his way, he could drive the way he wanted and force every car to catch him. Raikkonen was third in the standings. He still had a chance for the championship.

Montoya would start fourth. He was second in the standings. Schumacher started seventh. Schumacher knew he had a difficult task ahead of himself. The race was on the course inside the giant oval track. It had twisting chicanes, or turns built into the road to limit speed. Passing is difficult on the winding Formula One courses. It became even more difficult as heavy rains fell throughout the race.

But Schumacher soon showed why he was a champion, and why he would be again.

Schumacher resisted the urge to push too hard when the track was covered in water. He remained patient as Raikkonen and other drivers swapped the lead. In wet conditions, proper tires are especially important. Drivers with tires made for a dry track began sliding, slowing, and losing their positions. Drivers with the correct tires for the wet conditions had better control of their cars. Schumacher waited for the right time to duck into the pits and have the proper tires put on his Ferrari.

Smart planning, a fast car, and a skilled driver are all important for winning. Everything was all coming together for Schumacher on this rainy day.

Schumacher was driving very well in the wet conditions. The race would last 73 laps. He began climbing the leaderboard on Lap 21. Soon Jenson Button from England was the only man left between Schumacher and the checkered flag. But Schumacher remained patient. He waited for the right moment to strike.

Schumacher raced down the front stretch of the racecourse. He pulled even with Button on Lap 37. On Lap 38, he entered the first turn and thrust his Ferrari into the lead. The fans in the stands roared. It was almost all over.

Schumacher pulled away. He had such a comfortable lead that Raikkonen could not even think of catching him. The race and the pursuit of the championship were all but over. Schumacher would later call it "one of the best days of my life."

Schumacher showed patience and cunning strategy that day. The victory swung the championship battle in Schumacher's favor. He whipped the entire field of world-class drivers. Some observers argued it was the most impressive race of his legendary career.

Schumacher went to the final race of the season in Japan as the championship leader. He won his sixth title. That moved

Michael Schumacher celebrates his 2003 US Grand Prix victory.

him past Juan Manuel Fangio atop the all-time list. He was the

greatest champion in the history of the most popular type of

racing in the world.

Formula One is a worldwide passion for millions of fans.

The word *formula* means a set of rules that govern the

competition. The sport began as an unorganized group of

drivers who raced some of the earliest automobiles in the

1900s. It has developed into one of the most popular sports in the world.

Formula One, or F1, is part auto race and part international sensation. The cars feature open wheels. That means the wheels are on the outside of the car's body. That helps the car sit lower to the ground. A lower profile limits wind resistance and increases speed. The cars race on tracks all around the world in exotic locations and huge, glamorous cities. Some tracks are enclosed within huge stadiums. Others races are held on road courses. In these races, cars speed through city streets that have been closed off to the public.

Formula One races are based on distance, not laps. Each track is shaped differently. That means a lap at one track might be longer than a lap at another track. But each race is roughly 305 kilometers (km) (190 miles) long. So a race might last 73 laps, like in Indianapolis. Or it might last only 66 laps, as in Barcelona, Spain.

Sebastian Vettel celebrates after winning a race in Brazil in 2013. He also won the 2013 season championship as the top Formula One driver in the world.

The Formula One season consists of a series of Grand Prix races. That term is French for "great prize." The number of races each season has increased over the years. The 2013 season consisted of 19 Grand Prix races. They were held on five continents over eight months.

Two champions are crowned each year. One championship goes to the best driver. The other goes to the best car manufacturer. Points are determined by the order of finish in each race. To be a champion is to be a legend, forever. Just like Michael Schumacher.

chapter 2

STARTING SMALL

Some have said that the first automobile race was held as soon as the second car was built. It almost worked out that way. The first patent for an automobile was awarded in 1886. Men began racing their clunky, primitive vehicles in Europe as early as 1894. Drivers in business suits and dress hats began testing themselves and their machines on courses cutting through the European countryside. The cars were not fast by modern standards. They had wooden

Auto racing has been a popular sport since cars were invented.

wheels and crude, gasoline-powered engines. Races were won at 16 miles per hour (mph) or 25 kilometers per hour (km/h). But the races were thrilling and became very popular.

In 1904 the Fédération Internationale de l'Automobile was formed in Paris, France. It aimed to set common rules for all the races that were popping up everywhere. Common rules would make the races fairer. They also would allow the sport of racing to grow. Cars were quickly becoming faster and more reliable. The passion for racing cars was on the rise.

Soon Europeans began hatching ideas for a large racing series to span the continent. These plans were made for many years. However, World War I (1914–1918) and World War II (1939–1945) prevented any attempts to begin racing. Europe was left in ruins twice. No one had the time or the money to run organized races during this period.

By 1946, however, the roots of what would become modern Formula One were in place. The manufacturers and drivers came together to create a new organization. All cars

Legendary driver Juan Manuel Fangio races in the Swiss Grand Prix in 1954.

and drivers had to follow the same set of rules, or formula. The first official race was held in Pau, France.

From the beginning, Formula One was a dangerous sport. Many drivers were injured or killed in crashes. The technology to keep them safe was decades behind the ability to make cars go faster and stop quickly. Fans often were harmed too.

But the public was fascinated by these brave or foolish men who careened around the race courses. Danger was part of the thrill. Men such as Sir Stirling Moss and Juan Manuel Fangio became heroes.

Racing also was of great interest to new automobile companies such as Ferrari, Mercedes-Benz, and Alfa Romeo. Racing gave companies a perfect way to test out how fast or how tough their cars were. Fans wanted to drive vehicles manufactured by the companies that built winning race cars. And everyone loved a winner. Ferrari was among the first to benefit. The Italian company has a long and successful history in Formula One. Ferrari is the only manufacturer that has competed since the first year of the series.

A Ferrari ready to race in 1964

Rules for the engines, tires, and cars have changed often
and still do. Arguments over rules continue today. Some fans
cheer for certain manufacturers. Some fans root for the drivers
themselves. Others like drivers from certain countries. But the
best racers still stand out because of their driving skill.

The road course in Monaco is a longtime favorite of drivers and fans.

The series took a huge step toward becoming the most popular type of auto racing in the world in 1978. That year, a businessman named Bernie Ecclestone became president of the Formula One Constructors Association, the group that has governed the series since 1974. Under his leadership, Formula One improved safety measures to protect drivers. He also helped set up new television contracts that allowed fans around the world to watch the races.

Those racing pioneers driving cars with wooden wheels could never have imagined what they started.

chapter 3

ROCKET SHIPS ON EARTH

Formula One car is basically similar to a car you might see on the street. But every part of it has been tweaked to make the car faster. Wheels sit outside the body of the car. Wings on the front and back make the cars more aerodynamic. The cockpit has only one seat. Most of these differences make the cars lighter. A lighter car with a powerful engine can go really fast.

Formula One cars are built for speed.

The sleek race cars used in Formula One are some of the most researched and developed machines on the planet. Teams spend millions of dollars to design and build them to gain every advantage within the rules. The series has tried to limit how much money can be spent. But the participants have resisted. Teams felt a $40 million limit proposed in 2010 was too low. They are still free to spend as much as they wish.

Cars can be no more than 70.8 inches (180 centimeters) wide. Almost every curve and bump has a measurement that must not be exceeded. These measurements are checked against templates that all cars must match. Each team's cars look alike because the rules are so strict. Engineers pore over every inch of the cars' bodies looking for advantages.

Ready for Takeoff

Fans rarely get to see a Formula One car go full out. That is because Formula One racecourses rarely have straightaways. The cars certainly have the potential to go fast, though. They can reach well beyond 200 mph (322 km/h) and accelerate like rockets. In 2005 a British American Racing Honda set an unofficial record with a 256 mph (412 km/h) run in a straight-line test.

Drivers have to handle tight curves in Formula One races.

The cars must weigh at least 1,521 pounds (690 kilograms) at all times. That total includes the driver's weight, but not the weight of the fuel.

Rules even limit how the wings on the back and nose of the cars can be used to improve the aerodynamics of the car. Drivers can adjust the wings at times to help the car stick to the track. The aim is to create what is called downforce.

Wings on the front and back of the car help improve its aerodynamics.

Formula One engines run on gasoline similar to that used in regular cars. The engines can have a capacity of no more than 1.6 liters and eight cylinders. The cars also use the Energy Recovery System to capture energy created when the car brakes. The system converts that energy into boost power to generate even more speed.

Every driver in the sport wants a fast race car. Many want a car that looks stylish. But safety is still important. The cars can easily go 200 mph (321 km/h) and can hit 60 mph (96 km/h) in about two seconds. Protecting the driver in these conditions is difficult but important. Helmets and restraint systems have improved over the years to help keep drivers safe.

Safety First

Drivers have been required to wear helmets in Formula One since 1953. However, accidents often have shown how they need to be improved. New technology and materials have made them better. Modern helmets must be light and tough. They are made from carbon fiber and a material glued together in layers.

Driving a car that runs on explosive fuel has been a worry since racing began. The fuel tank is actually a flexible bladder that resists crushing. That keeps fuel from spreading onto the track, where it can catch fire. Panels that resist crushing also

surround the cockpit. Roll bars in front and behind the cockpit protect the driver's head in case the car flips.

But even the best machine will not run at peak performance without a skilled operator at the wheel.

1. **TIRES:** Made from various types of rubber to offer differences in durability and performance.

2. **DIFFUSER:** The rear section of the car's underside where air passes through. It helps make the car more aerodynamic.

3. **MONOCOQUE:** The single-piece core of the car, where the cockpit is located. The engine sits behind it.

4. **SIDEPOD:** Flanks the monocoque to the rear wing and houses the radiators.

5. **ROLL BAR:** Metal hoop behind the headrest that protects a driver in case of a rollover.

6. **FRONT WING:** Increases traction and speed by pushing the wind rushing onto the car down onto the track.

7. **COCKPIT:** Seating area for driver where all controls are located.

chapter 4

ATHLETES IN THE COCKPIT

The cockpit of a Formula One race car is one of the most demanding places in sports. The high speeds and quick cornering of the cars jostle drivers' bodies. Racing is much more physical than it appears. Driving a Formula One car is more than just sitting and turning a wheel.

Drivers are seat-belted snuggly, but their bodies still suffer great stress and strain from

A driver sits in the cockpit of a Formula One race car.

Drivers are under a lot of pressure during a race.

tugging and pulling. The effects are similar to what astronauts or fighter pilots can experience.

This stress requires drivers to be physically fit. Many drivers are not very tall. But they must be strong. And they must have great endurance to maintain that strength through a long race. Special care is taken to strengthen neck muscles. The drivers' heavy helmets and the forces that push against them during sharp corners can cause great strain.

Drivers can sweat off more than six pounds (2.7 kg) in one race. Drivers and their doctors work hard to prevent dehydration. That is when a body is low on fluids. Drivers begin hydrating by taking in large amounts of water early in the week before a race.

Drivers work hard to stay fit. They do cardio workouts to make their hearts stronger. They also lift weights to build their muscles. A driver's heartbeat can reach an incredible 190 beats per minute during a race. A normal resting heartbeat is between 60 and 100. Being able to control their breathing and muscles takes great effort.

Learning the Ropes

Drivers do not begin racing at the Formula One level. Most begin racing in a feeder system, the training ground for future Formula One drivers. From 1985 to 2004, less experienced racers competed in the Formula 3000 series. Since 2005 the GP2 series has taken over as the top feeder series. Most races are held on the same tracks as Formula One races.

Every bit of food drivers eat is planned out to provide the best possible nutrition.

The cockpit of a Formula One car has been described as one of the loudest workplaces on earth. Noise levels reach 85 times the recommended level. This is similar to standing next to the speakers at a rock concert. Drivers and their crews wear special ear plugs to block out as much noise as possible.

It takes a special person to be able to handle the pressure of driving a Formula One car. To be the best, a driver needs both a strong body and a sharp mind.

chapter 5

FORMULA ONE SUPERSTARS

F ormula One has a long history of producing successful drivers who became heroes to a legion of fans.

Juan Manuel Fangio of Argentina was dominant in the early years of Formula One. He claimed five of the first 10 championships. He was nicknamed El Maestro in Spanish. That means "The Master." He lived up to that nickname. Fangio won an incredible 24 times in 51 races. He is the oldest driver

Argentinian Juan Manuel Fangio was one of the pioneers of Formula One racing.

to win a championship. He was 46 years, 41 days old when he won his last Formula One title in 1957. His record of five championships lasted for 46 years.

One of Fangio's top rivals was Sir Stirling Moss of Great Britain. He won 16 Grand Prix races. Moss was called the greatest driver never to win a world championship. That is both a good and bad thing. Moss finished second in the standings every year from 1955 to 1958. The first three times he was second to Fangio, his teammate on the Mercedes team. In 1958 Moss was second by just one point. Moss retired from high-speed racing in 1962 after a crash left him in a coma for a month.

Alain Prost of France was one of the most successful and controversial figures in Formula One history. Prost won 51 races and four championships. His ability to win races was matched only by his ability to win and lose fans and friends. Prost raced for four teams in his career despite his success.

Prost had a long feud with the very popular Brazilian driver Ayrton Senna. That made Prost even less popular.

Senna was perhaps the most popular driver in Formula One history. He was also three-time champion. His death at age 34 after an accident at the Imola course in Italy in 1994 shocked and saddened millions. Senna was known as a generous and thoughtful champion. He was beloved at home in Brazil. He donated millions of dollars to charities there. Senna was fascinated by what it took to reach the limits of drivers and machines. He has remained popular years

Other Trailblazers

While the Formula One driver roster continues to be dominated by white men, there have been notable breakthroughs. Lewis Hamilton of England is a black driver whose family comes from the island nation of Grenada. He won the 2008 championship for McLaren in just his second season. Only five women have entered a Grand Prix since 1950 and two qualified to compete in the race. Maria Theresa de Filippis of Italy made three starts in 1958. Fellow Italian Lella Lombardi became the only woman to earn points in a Formula One race in the 1975 Spanish Grand Prix.

Brazilian Ayrton Senna was one of the most popular drivers in Formula One history.

after his death. Many professional race car drivers call him their inspiration.

After Senna's death, Michael Schumacher became the most famous Formula One driver in the world. He also is the most successful driver in the history of Formula One. The German holds series records for championships (seven), wins (91), poles (68), and virtually anything else a driver would want. Schumacher retired after the 2006 season at age 37. But he made a successful comeback in 2010. He has never been the most beloved. But he has always been respected. He is known for his tremendous work ethic. And the results of his work have always showed.

Fellow German Sebastian Vettel took over for Schumacher as the face of Formula One. In 2010 at age 23, he became the youngest racer ever to win a Formula One title. He matched Schumacher's record of 13 wins in 2013. He claimed his fourth title in 2013 for Red Bull Racing and continues to set records.

GLOSSARY

AERODYNAMICS
How air flowing around a car can affect its speed and handling.

CARBON FIBER
A material consisting of thin, strong crystalline filaments of carbon, used as a strengthening material.

CHICANE
An artificial turn or corner built into a racecourse to force drivers to slow down, generally for safety reasons.

COCKPIT
The driver's compartment of a race car, containing a molded seat, headrest, steering wheel, and electronic instruments. In Formula One cars, it is protected by a roll bar but no roof.

DOWNFORCE
The combination of resistance and gravity that keeps cars on the ground. This downward thrust is created by aerodynamics. It is especially important in turns.

PATENT
An inventor's exclusive right to manufacture an item.

POLE POSITION
The first car in line at the start of a race.

QUALIFYING LAP
A timed lap run before each race to determine the starting order of the drivers.

ROLL BAR
A reinforced metal hoop fastened behind a driver's head to prevent it from hitting the ground if the race car flips.

FOR MORE INFORMATION

Further Readings

Allen, James. *Michael Schumacher: The Edge of Greatness*. London, UK: Headline, 2008.

Arron, Mark and Mark Hughes. *The Complete Book of Formula One*. Minneapolis, MN: MBI, 2008.

Chimits, Xavier. *Grand Prix Racers: Portraits of Speed*. Minneapolis, MN: MBI, 2008.

Folley, Malcolm. *Senna Versus Prost*. London, UK: Arrow, 2010.

Tibballs, Geoff. *Motor Racing's Strangest Races*. London, UK: Portico, 2012.

Websites

To learn more about Inside the Speedway, visit **booklinks.abdopublishing.com**. These links are routinely monitored and updated to provide the most current information available.

INDEX

About the Author

Brant James has written for SI.com, *USA Today*, and ESPN.com. His adventures covering fast cars and daring racers have taken him from the Indianapolis 500 and Daytona 500 to the flight deck of the USS *Theodore Roosevelt*. He lives in Florida with his wife and son.